Step by Step

Meditations on Wisdom and Compassion

Step by Step

Maha Ghosananda

Edited by
Jane Sharada Mahoney
and Philip Edmonds

Parallax Press
Berkeley, California

Parallax Press
P.O. Box 7355
Berkeley, CA 94707

Proceeds from the sale of this book will help purchase complimentary editions of *Step by Step* to be distributed to Cambodians worldwide.

Cover and book design by Ayelet Maida
Cover photograph by Don Farber
Page 25 photograph by Judith Canty
Page 49 photograph courtesy of *Providence Journal-Bulletin*
Page 80 photograph by Jonathan Sharlin

Library of Congress Cataloging-in-Publication Data
Ghosananda, Maha, 1929-
   Step by step : meditations on wisdom and compassion / Maha Ghosananda ; edited by Jane Sharada Mahoney and Philip Edmonds.
      p.   cm.
   ISBN 0-938077-43-0 (pbk.) : $9.00
   1. Buddhism--Doctrines. 2. Religious life--Buddhism. I. Mahoney, Jane Sharada. II. Edmonds, Philip. III. Title.
BQ4165.G48 1991
294.3'42--dc20   91-32829
                                                 CIP

Contents

Meditations on Compassion

Preface
by Jack Kornfield

Since I met him more than twenty years ago, Maha Ghosananda has represented to me the essence of sweet generosity and unstoppable courage of heart. Just to be in his presence, to experience his smile and the infectious loving kindness that flows from him is healing to the spirit.

I have seen Maha Ghosananda in many circumstances: practicing as a forest monk, as a father figure for Cambodian children, as a translator and scholar of fifteen languages, as a meditation master for Western students, as a peacemaker at the United Nations, and as one of the living treasures of Cambodia leading the Khmer refugee communities around the world. In these situations, his heart has remained unfalteringly compassionate and joyful, and he emanates the teachings of simplicity and love. He would and has offered the robes off his back and the food in his bowl to anyone who needs them.

Some years ago, in the dusty, barren heat of Cambodian refugee camps that hold hundreds of thousands of shell-shocked survivors, I saw the greatness of Maha Ghosananda's heart and the Buddha's shine as one. In the camps of the Khmer Rouge, where people were warned not to cooperate at the cost of their lives, Maha Ghosananda opened a Buddhist temple. He wanted to bring the Dharma back to these people who had suffered as deeply as any on Earth. In spite of the threats, when the large bamboo temple was completed, nearly 20,000 refugees gathered to recite again the lost chants of 2,000 years—left behind when their own villages were burned and temples destroyed. Maha Ghosananda chanted to them the traditional chants as thousands wept.

Then it was time to speak, to proclaim the holy Dharma, to bring the teachings of the Buddha to bear witness to the unspeakable sorrows of their lives. Maha Ghosananda spoke with utmost simplicity to those who had suffered, reciting over and over in the ancient language of the Buddha and in Cambodian this verse from the *Dhammapada:*

> *Hatred never ceases by hatred*
> *but by love alone is healed.*
> *This is the ancient and eternal law.*

It is this eternal spirit that flows through Maha Ghosananda. If he could come out of this book, he would smile at you or laugh with sparkling joy. Because he cannot, you will find him in these words, the quiet simplicity and truth that underlie his loving presence.

Enjoy these blessings.

Spirit Rock Center
Woodacre, California
November 1991

Foreword
by Dith Pran

On the morning of April 17, 1975, Cambodians welcomed the victorious Khmer Rouge troops with flowers, bowls of rice, and cheers. But the next day, as the soldiers brutally forced us out of our homes and onto a long march into the countryside, our hearts filled with terror, and I watched my homeland plunge into darkness.

In the painful years to come we witnessed the dismantling of our society and the desecration of most all that we cherished. Rigid collectivization, forced labor, and harsh rules controlled every part of our lives; we lost our freedom, our possessions, our family lives, and our centuries-old Buddhist tradition. The Killing Fields—acres of mass graves and exposed bodies outside nearly every village—were gruesome reminders that our lives depended upon the ability to please our captors. During those dark years, I witnessed some of the most ignoble horrors and unfathomable brutalities ever known to humankind.

Wondrously, out of this devastation came a leader of great calm and compassion, the Venerable Maha Ghosananda. Where the revolution had produced division, this serene monk saw the chance for reconciliation; where there had been violence, Ghosananda saw the potential for kindness. He called this the Law of Opposites.

Maha Ghosananda is the dreamkeeper of Cambodia. He has dedicated his life to the celebration and nurturance of the best in our culture, and in all of human culture. Although his entire family was lost in the holocaust, he shows no bitterness. He is a symbol of Cambodian Buddhism, personifying the gentleness, forbearance, compassion, and peacefulness of the Buddha—qualities that Cambodians have always honored.

Ghosananda's unyielding faith in Cambodia's ability to heal itself has encouraged us in our quest for cultural and spiritual rebirth and our desperate struggle for peace. His luminous presence and wise counsel at the highest levels of peace talks have reminded the country's four warring factions of humanitarian goals that transcend self-interest. Maha Ghosananda constantly reminds us that national peace can only begin with personal peace.

The Khmer Rouge declared religious practice a capital offense. What they did not understand was that no degree of violence or repression could ever kill Buddhism at its source—our people's deep love for the tradition. Since those dark years, Maha Ghosananda has worked ceaselessly to restore Cambodian Buddhism—training monks and nuns and building temples all over the world. He is always rekindling the spiritual spark the Khmer Rouge tried to extinguish.

In the Fall of 1975, after six months of life under the Khmer Rouge, I secretly forayed into a collective paddy to gather a handful of rice to relieve my hunger. A cadre witnessed this crime and ordered my punishment. Angry young soldiers pummeled me with bladed harvest tools and tethered me to a tree for the night. Kneeling and bleeding in the mud and rain, my arms tied tightly behind my back, I feared my execution would come the next day.

I prayed to myself that I might live to see my wife and children again. Somehow the Khmer Rouge released me two days later, and, my heart filled with reverence, I shaved my head in the traditional Buddhist gesture of thankfulness. I did not care that this might bring on more punishment. Ironically, the Khmer Rouge accepted my explanation that I had removed my hair to relieve migraines!

Throughout the time of fear, our Buddhist tradition sustained us. We prayed in silence—burning candles to help guide the spirits of those who had died, to express gratitude for life's small blessings, and to search for the strength to face another day. But rebuilding our faith after the Khmer Rouge defeat proved an even greater challenge. Our country was in ruins—famine was everywhere, families were scattered, loved ones lost, and homes and villages destroyed. We were ill and tired, and, all too often, despair and depression overcame us. It was Maha Ghosananda who traveled to Cambodia, to the refugee camps in Thailand, and to Cambodian communities around the world reminding us that Buddhism was alive in us, and that we could call upon the sweetness and depth of the tradition. Ghosananda's quest has been the journey of a hero. He has reminded us by his own example to take each step slowly, carefully, and in mindfulness, and to always continue on.

Now, after decades of conflict, Cambodia's warring factions have signed a peace agreement. Finally, we can see the opportunity to heal years of bitter conflict—to create a Cambodia that celebrates sovereignty, human rights, self-determination, and freedom from the special interests

of larger powers. With awareness and courage, we can rebuild a Cambodia that is safe and strong for our children.

Maha Ghosananda's teachings—simple in character,
but most profound in impact—can help guide us on our
way. His essential message, that great suffering contains
the seeds of wisdom, compassion, and peace, offers price-
less hope and consolation, not only for Cambodia, but for
the whole world.

Brooklyn, New York
October 24, 1991

Step by Step

Editors' Introduction

Rarely in human history has a nation been so embroiled in war, autogenocide, forced labor, social engineering, and self-destruction as Cambodia in the late twentieth century. A small tropical country, wedged precariously on the Southeast Asian peninsula between Thailand, Laos, Vietnam, and the South China Sea, Cambodia's history dates back 2,000 years. From the ninth to the thirteenth centuries, known as the Angkor Period or "Golden Age," Cambodian (or Khmer) kings controlled vast portions of the Indochinese peninsula, and led an empire marked by scientific, cultural, and religious achievements. During other periods, Cambodia fluctuated between independence and being dominated by neighboring states and other foreign governments.

In the mid-nineteenth century the country was colonized by France, becoming part of French Indochina. To insure domestic peace, the French allowed the Khmer kings to remain as symbolic leaders. In 1953, after a century of colonial rule, King Norodom Sihanouk peacefully negotiated Cambodia's independence. In accordance with the sovereignty agreement, the king abdicated his throne and declared himself a candidate for popular election. With overwhelming popular regard for the Khmer royal lineage, the people elected Sihanouk to be head of state and he assumed the title of Prince. For the next decade, Cambodia enjoyed independence, peace, and prosperity.

By the mid-1960s, North Vietnamese troops had begun establishing hidden sanctuaries in the Cambodian countryside. Prince Sihanouk, citing increased American activity in Vietnam and accusing the U.S. of making border incursions into Cambodia, a neutral country, severed economic and military relations with the United States.

In 1969, the U.S. began bombing the Cambodian countryside to destroy North Vietnamese military installations and supply lines. The bombing wreaked havoc on the country's rural population and agrarian economy. Business, military, and intellectual groups began harshly criticizing Prince Sihanouk's policies, and in 1970, while Sihanouk traveled abroad, there was a bloodless coup, ending the centuries-old lineage of monarchs. Lon Nol, a general who had the backing of the Americans, was named by the coup leaders to be head of state.

The new government quickly drafted a formal alliance with the U.S., and the bombings increased in frequency and magnitude. In May 1970, American ground forces invaded Cambodia, killing and wounding civilians and destroying marketplaces, ricefields, and villages in their search for Vietnamese Communists.

The continued bombing, along with the ending of the traditional monarchy, widened the political rift between Cambodia's rural and urban classes. The peasants, who had held the royalty in the highest esteem, found Lon Nol's policies to be ill-conceived and exploitative. In their disenfranchisement lay the seeds of a revolution that would change Cambodia forever.

An indigenous Communist movement had been brewing in Cambodia since the early 1930s. Led by young urban intellectuals, many of whom had studied in Paris along with the Vietnamese Communists, the party saw the growing discontent of the rural population as an opportunity to put their ultra-Marxist theories into practice. As the party's ranks swelled with disaffected peasants and farmers as well as rural adolescents, Prince Sihanouk joined them, and he became their titular head. With this sudden credibility, the Khmer Rouge—as the party came to be known—attracted vital arms support from China. Solath Sar, a young scholar, assumed the leadership, although his identity was hidden from the public. Years later, he was introduced only under his *nom de guerre,* Pol Pot.

Aerial attacks forced the North Vietnamese troops deeper and deeper into Cambodia, and they allied themselves with the Khmer Rouge to combat the pro-American forces of Lon Nol. The countryside became decimated, and once-prosperous farmers had to forage for food in order to survive. Thousands fled the villages for the security of Phnom Penh, Battambang, and other urban areas.

The U.S. military action in Cambodia ended in August 1973, but the civil war continued. The Khmer Rouge took control of an increasing number of towns and villages, often ingratiating themselves to the villagers by launching elaborate civic projects, praising Buddhism, and vilifying Lon Nol.

By the Spring of 1975, Cambodia's cities were in a state of crisis, overwhelmed by the influx of villagers that had tripled their populations. Inflation raged, and displaced families and orphaned children wandered the streets, hopelessly searching for food, medicine, and shelter. Between 1967 and 1975, an estimated one million Cambodians were killed or wounded and two million left homeless. The country that had been known as "the ricebowl of Indochina" was now on the verge of famine.

On the morning of April 17, 1975, just two weeks before the North Vietnamese marched into Saigon to end the Vietnam War, Khmer Rouge forces invaded Phnom Penh, and by mid-afternoon the Lon Nol forces had succumbed. Cheers rang through the streets, as many citizens believed that peace had come at last.

But the next day at dawn, the Khmer Rouge declared "Year Zero," the beginning of a new era, and began an extreme program of social reconstruction. All city dwellers, young and old, rich and poor, were to march to the countryside to live and work as peasants.

"Take nothing with you," the soldiers insisted. "*Angka* [the Khmer Rouge organization] will provide." Frightened and bewildered, most people obeyed. Many who tried to gather cooking pots, heirlooms, personal items, or foodstuffs were shot. Hospital patients who were too sick to walk were hurled from windows. As tensions grew, the Khmer Rouge soldiers offered false encouragement. "You will return in three days. These are only temporary measures." More than three million citizens of all ages were marched to rural communes, and thousands died of heat, exhaustion, thirst, dysentery, and stress.

"Year Zero" and Pol Pot's ultra-Marxism were to be the basis of another glorious "golden age." Angka (not to be confused with Angkor, the ancient empire) sought to create a self-reliant, pure, classless, agrarian culture. Cities were to be abolished; jungles and fallow fields were to be reclaimed, using elaborate irrigation systems to multiply agricultural yields. The new egalitarian utopia would erase all vestiges of modernization and Western influence. To realize these goals, the Khmer Rouge isolated their country under a thick veil of secrecy. Roads on the border were secured and communication was severed.

The Khmer Rouge removed Prince Sihanouk from titular power and placed him under house arrest. The country was divided into eight sectors with authority for governance delegated to the eight section leaders. Interpretation of ideology and harshness of discipline varied from sector to sector. Each citizen was assigned to a work unit. Traditional peasant dress of loosely-fitting black pajamas and shortly-cropped hair became the norm for all ages and both sexes.

Housing was assigned by Angka. Since the Khmer Rouge had razed many villages while seizing power, small huts were crafted from local materials. Typically, these shelters were built without walls to give Khmer Rouge cadres a clear view of household activities.

Manual labor replaced mechanization. All Cambodians became peasant laborers, regardless of age, health, skills, or former profession. Under guard, they silently cultivated fields with hoes and sickles, ox-carts, and water buffalo, or by hitching themselves to plows. Labor details extended up to eighteen hours per day, seven days a week. Children as young as three and the very elderly worked alongside able-bodied adults. "Those who work eat," was the inflexible motto. But the outdated farming methods soon produced insufficient rice yields, and food had to be rationed strictly—those who were ill and could not work received even less. As food supplies dwindled, desperate villagers secretly began to forage for roots, leaves, bark, insects, or rats, even though in some sectors the personal gathering of food was a punishable offense.

The Khmer Rouge designed irrigation systems that they hoped would rival the legendary waterworks of the Angkor kingdom. But without the aid of engineers or modern technology, the systems failed. Drinking water became infested, water for crops became scarce, and the already small harvests withered. Malnutrition and overwork took their toll. Starvation, dysentery, cholera, malaria, and stress-related illnesses abounded. Many villagers became blind from vitamin deficiency. Medical treatment was strictly rationed and limited to traditional folk methods.

To forge the Year Zero and their own control, the Khmer Rouge outlawed almost everything that evoked Cambodia's cultural foundations. Cambodia had been a land steeped in tradition, and among the strongest ties were those of the family. In many sectors, family life was abolished—children lived separately from parents, either in individual quarters or on work sites miles away. In many cases families lost all contact with one another.

Even in sectors where families remained intact, community concerns took precedence, and the traditional order of respect was inverted. Children, "unspoiled vessels of Angka," were granted authority over adults. Children could issue work assignments to adults and were encouraged to report on adults' violations of Angka's policies. Parents lost the right to choose mates for their children. Khmer Rouge cadres arranged and performed all marriages, and revolutionary ceremonies replaced Buddhist rituals. Weddings were often held in the fields so that work flow would not be interrupted. Young couples who met secretly without Angka's sanction were punished. In some instances, the naked corpses of young lovers were displayed in public places, offering a grim reminder not to challenge Angka.

Private lives and feelings remained under close scrutiny. One could be severely punished simply for complaining. In many instances people were forced to watch in silence as their loved ones were murdered, since to cry out would be to question Angka's judgment. Memories, too, were forbidden. Since Year Zero marked the dawn of new time, sentimental yearnings were considered to be a hindrance to progress. One could be punished for speaking of the Buddha, the king, or days gone by. Singing old songs or telling old tales was considered a crime against the state. "Angka is like a pineapple," people were told. "Its eyes can see in all directions."

"What is infected must be cut out," became the philosophy for social "purification." Those who challenged Angka's political position or those found to be from less than "pure" peasant stock were to be systematically eliminated. Singled out for extinction were members of former government and military operations, monks and nuns, ethnic minorities, and anyone who had received formal education. Executions often took place without trials. In extreme cases, fair skin, the wearing of eyeglasses, or speaking in a non-peasant dialect was sufficient cause for execution.

"To keep you is no profit, to destroy you is no loss," the Khmer Rouge declared. To survive, families shed their former identities and fabricated elaborate details of past residence, lifestyle, and profession. Doctors, lawyers, teachers, and business leaders feigned knowledge of farming, hoping to avoid the horror of mass execution. In severe cases, whole families, including infants, were killed and buried together in mass graves.

To enforce its power, Angka sponsored regular and involuntary indoctrinational sessions, called "educational meetings," to proclaim the glories of the state. At times villagers who had violated rules were paraded before meetings for public humiliation or corporal punishment. Thousands of "incorrigibles" were shipped to re-education centers and subjected to meager rations, hard labor, and torture. At Tuol Sleng, a former high school in Phnom Penh, thousands of photographs and detailed records provide evidence of over 12,000 deaths—men, women, and children hanged, drowned, disemboweled, mutilated, or electrocuted by Khmer Rouge cadres.

Only the poor, illiterate, and unskilled were left to work the land. Weakened by hunger and overwhelmed by the struggle for survival, they were unable to unite or to pose any significant resistance. Corpses and mass graves lay scattered around the outskirts of most villages. Cambodians began to call their homeland "The Killing Fields."

By 1978, a number of Khmer Rouge leaders had become disaffected and staged a series of unsuccessful coups. In response, Angka turned its persecutions inward, imprisoning thousands of former leaders at Tuol Sleng. Many fled to Vietnam for safety.

At the same time, the Khmer Rouge power was being threatened externally by Vietnamese invasions. Soon after seizing control of Phnom Penh, the Khmer Rouge had abandoned its military alliance with Vietnam and launched a series of attacks on Vietnam border sites. By late 1978, these isolated battles had become a full-scale guerrilla war that had spread into the Cambodian countryside. The Khmer Rouge conscripted thousands of Cambodian youths, some as young as ten. As the Vietnamese gained control of more Cambodian towns and villages, the Khmer Rouge fled to the mountains on the Thai border, burning farms, ricefields, and villages in their retreat. On Christmas Day, 1978, the Vietnamese forces, aided by a small contingent of Khmer Rouge dissidents, launched an attack on Phnom Penh, and on January 7, 1979, they seized control of the country.

With Vietnamese occupation, the full horror and destruction of Cambodia's Khmer Rouge years became known to the world. Two to three million Cambodians had died of starvation, disease, overwork, torture, and execution. Countless others were wounded and disabled, and would bear the physical and emotional scars of the holocaust for the rest of their lives. Families were scattered—many would never find their loved ones again. Orphans wandered alone, searching for protection. Homes and villages were razed, and corpses fouled the ricefields and roadways.

The country was in ruins. Hospitals, banks, industry, and government offices had been reduced to rubble. Abandoned vehicles littered deteriorated roadways and bridges. The currency had been abolished, commerce had ground to a halt, and educational and cultural institutions had disintegrated. Food was scarce, there was no electricity, and the only available water was contaminated. Survivors of the holocaust, their lives shattered, sought the strength to rebuild their lives and their nation.

*   *   *

In the North, the thunder roars—
Fire burns the water, the Bodhi tree,
*   and the jungle....*

This well-known Cambodian poem, called the "Buddha prophecy," was inscribed centuries ago on a thin palm leaf. Reading it in light of recent events, it seems to have foretold the near-destruction of Cambodian Buddhism during the Khmer Rouge era. Under Year Zero policies, almost all of Cambodia's 3,600 Buddhist temples were destroyed, and only an estimated 3,000 of Cambodia's 50,000 monks survived the persecution of hard labor, torture, starvation, and execution. There are no precise statistics on the fate of Cambodian Buddhist nuns, but the fact of their persecution is well-documented. Most Cambodian Buddhist archives and scriptures were desecrated as well.

The tigress always finds food in the jungle.
Even while asleep, she safeguards our religion....
When the sun goes down,
*   the tigress sets forth to extinguish the blaze.*

The "Buddha Prophecy" also seems to suggest hope. Maha Ghosananda has called it a celebration of the strength of the Cambodian Buddhist *sangha*, the community of monks. The "Bodhi tree," site of the Buddha's enlightenment, is a symbol for Buddhism. The "tigress," Ghosananda suggests, is a symbol of the Cambodians' deep love for Buddhism.

Founded in India in the sixth century B.C.E., Buddhism migrated to Cambodia during the latter half of the Angkor period. In the late twelfth century, Angkorian King Jayavarman VII declared Buddhism the state religion, and since then it has endured as the native religion of most Cambodians.

The vast majority of Cambodians are of Khmer descent, and it is often said with pride, "To be Khmer is to be Buddhist," although, of course, there are Cambodians who follow other religious traditions. In the countryside, Buddhist practice often embraces a syncretic blend of animism and indigenous spirit worship. Over the years, Buddhism has played a central role in Cambodian society, serving as a blueprint for everyday life, a moral structure, a guide for family life, a basis for national holidays and cultural events, and a foundation for social policy.

There has always been a reciprocal relationship between the monks and the laity. In keeping with their vows, the renunciants own no personal property, consume only the food offered them on their daily almsrounds, wear only robes given by laypersons, and depend on donated funds for all temple expenses. In return, monks exemplify and uphold the moral standards for society, and perform vital services such as teaching and conducting rituals. As symbols of spiritual attainment, communal unity, and cultural pride, the monks are among the most highly respected members of Khmer society. The honored relationship between monks and the laity is intimately linked to the concept of "merit." By performing their reciprocal roles, both monks and the laity earn merit and work toward their respective goals of enlightenment and a favorable rebirth.

But the Khmer Rouge saw the monks as parasites, living at the expense of the masses. (This is similar to China's description of "pre-liberation" Tibetan Buddhism.) Angka believed that money given for the support of monks and nuns squandered the common wealth and compromised the economic livelihood of the country. The Khmer Rouge credo, "Those who work eat," was used to justify abolishing the monastic system.

Many monks who were not executed were given work assignments that required degrading labor, such as shoveling dung. Others were forced to perform traditionally forbidden tasks, such as transporting weapons. Temples (*wats*) were not only closed but desecrated. Most were demolished, and their bricks and iron were used to build roads, bridges, and foundations. Wats that were not leveled were transformed into ammunition storage sites, granaries, stables for livestock, pig farms, or manure dumps for the manufacture of fertilizer. Some temples in remote areas were used as torture and execution sites. As the temples were destroyed, statues of the Buddha were smashed, beheaded, or used for target practice. Ancient scriptures were burned, cast into ponds, or used as rolling paper for cigarettes.

"The Khmer Rouge believed they could kill Buddhism," Maha Ghosananda says. "They tried to stamp it out.... But Buddhism cannot die. Buddhism lives in Cambodian life, language, and love for ancestors. Most of all, Buddhism lives deeply in Cambodian hearts!"

*   *   *

The Venerable Maha Ghosananda was born in 1929 in the fertile plains of the Mekong Delta, into a farming clan in a small village of Takeo Province. At the age of eight, he began serving as temple boy in his village wat. The monks were impressed by his keen interest in monastic life, and they offered him much encouragement. When he was fourteen, Ghosananda asked for his parents' blessing to become a monk, and it was granted.

After graduating from the Buddhist University in Phnom Penh, Maha Ghosananda took up advanced studies at the Buddhist University of Battambang. He then left the country to complete his doctoral program at Nalanda University in Bihar, India, where he passed his Pali exams and received the title "Maha" before reaching the age of thirty. His name, Maha Ghosananda, means "Great Joyful Proclaimer."

To complement his university training, the monk visited Buddhist centers throughout Asia, studying with some of Buddhism's greatest contemporary masters. In Rajgir, India, Ghosananda became a student of the Japanese monk Nichidatsu Fujii, founder of the Nipponzan Myohoji sect devoted to world peace. It was from Master Fujii, a close associate of Mahatma Gandhi, that Ghosananda received his training in the skills of peace and nonviolence. He also received training from the late

Somdech Prah Sangha Raja Chuon Noth, the Supreme Patriarch of Cambodian Buddhism. Few monks receive the honor of discipleship with the Sangha Raja; to be accepted as a student of the patriarch is an honor and testimony to young Ghosananda's spiritual progress. Through his extensive travels and studies, Maha Ghosananda became fluent in Hindi, Bengali, Sanskrit, Pali, Sinhalese, Burmese, Vietnamese, Laotian, Thai, Japanese, French, English, German, and several Chinese dialects.

In 1965, at the age of thirty-six, Maha Ghosananda left Cambodia and journeyed to the isolated forests of southern Thailand, where he became a disciple of the noted meditation master, Achaan Dhammadaro. Today, when Maha Ghosananda demonstrates his meditation discipline to his students, he moves his left hand up and down in a slow, rhythmic motion, and says, "In the monastery we learned to meditate this way. All day long, we moved the hand up and down, up and down, with mindfulness, following each breath carefully. Every day, we did only this—nothing more." The life of meditation was well suited to this "natural monk."

Maha Ghosananda had been in the monastery just four years when the United States began bombing his country, and a full-scale ground war broke out the next year. "They told us, don't let Cambodia's suffering imprint on your minds. Do not let it disturb your concentration. Still," he says, "we cried for Cambodia every day."

But he remained in his Thai forest retreat for nine more years, as the war and then holocaust in Cambodia raged. Practicing mindful meditation, Ghosananda's inner peace grew, and he waited and prayed for a chance to help his people.

The dusty road to Sakeo was teeming with war-torn refugees. Under the scorching sun, streams of men and women, elders and children—bodies thin and broken, eyes sunken, faces baked and cracked from heat and exposure—wove their way along the dry, red earth. They staggered from exhaustion and wept from thirst, moving slowly and haltingly.

It was 1978. These were the survivors of the Killing Fields, fleeing the horrors of war, forced labor, genocide, and religious repression in Cambodia. Behind them were the ashes of their beloved cities and villages, ricefields and temples. Ahead were refugee camps and the hope for survival.

Fifty miles away, on a steep, winding pass, an ancient bus creaked its way down the mountain. Maha Ghosananda was perched cross-legged on a rigid seat with his head bowed, his eyes closed, and his saffron robe draping gracefully to the floor. The slightly-built, middle-aged monk appeared serene, unaffected by the exhaust fumes, the screeching tires, and the frequent lurching movements around him. Overflowing with compassion, Maha Ghosananda was making his way toward Sakeo Camp. One of just a few thousand Cambodian monks who had not perished under the Khmer Rouge, he traveled alone, arriving at Sakeo's gates three days after the first refugees.

The camp was stark—streets were crowded, sewage flowed in open gutters, food and water were scarce, and most refugees huddled inside their tattered cloth tents. Passing through the checkpoint, Ghosananda walked slowly toward the center of the camp, and as he did so the gloom that had enveloped the camp instantly turned to excitement. Refugees rushed to gaze at his saffron robe, the long-forbidden symbol of Buddhist devotion. Many peered from a safe distance, overwhelmed with anxious memories. Ghosananda reached into his cloth shoulder bag and pulled out a handful of tattered pamphlets— copies of the *Metta Sutta*, the Buddha's words of compassion and forgiveness for the oppressor. He offered one to each refugee within reach, bowing his head in the traditional gesture of respect.

In that moment, great suffering and great love merged. Centuries of Buddhist devotion rushed into the consciousness of the refugees. Waves of survivors fell to their knees and prostrated, wailing loudly, their cries reverberating throughout the camp. Many say that the Dharma, which had slept gently in their hearts as the Bodhi tree burned, was reawakened that day.

Since that first visit to Sakeo, Maha Ghosananda has worked tirelessly for peace and for the rebuilding of Cambodia. Following the example of the Buddha, all of Ghosananda's efforts have begun and ended with loving kindness, the force that he believes is powerful enough to "overcome the world."

*   *   *

Following their defeat of the Khmer Rouge, the Vietnamese established a puppet government in Cambodia, led by Heng Samrin, a Khmer Rouge defector. The Khmer Rouge army, which had been defeated but not decimated, regrouped at its mountain sanctuary in the northwest and soon posed a formidable resistance to Vietnamese control. Two additional resistance forces also emerged—one led by the former Prince Sihanouk and the other by Son Sann, Sihanouk's ex-prime minister. Each of the four factions built guerrilla forces, and they fought for control of Cambodia. In 1982, under pressure from China, the U.S., and other countries, the three Cambodian resistance forces allied to form a government-in-exile. The United Nations declared the Vietnamese-backed government to be an "occupation by force of arms" and awarded Cambodia's UN seat to the government-in-exile, which included the Khmer Rouge.

In late 1989, succumbing to years of pressure from the U.S., Vietnam withdrew its troops from Cambodia and installed Hun Sen, another Khmer Rouge defector, as head of government. In October 1991, in Paris, all four Cambodian factions signed a UN-brokered peace treaty, ending more than twenty-five years of warfare. According to the agreement, a ceasefire will be followed by a seventy percent demobilization of the four rival armies, the halting of foreign military support, the repatriation of nearly half a million refugees from the border camps, an interim government composed of representatives of the four factions and supervised by the United Nations, and UN-supervised elections to take place by mid-1993. The treaty confirms Cambodia's independence, sovereignty, and neutrality.

For more than ten years Maha Ghosananda has played an important role in helping bring about this long-awaited accord. His work as a diplomat and a spiritual and cultural leader behind the scenes has kept him traveling constantly from Cambodia to the refugee camps to the Cambodian resettlement communities worldwide. Beginning with Sakeo, Ghosananda established temples at each of the camps, including those controlled by the Khmer Rouge. He assisted the camp leaders in building spiritual, educational, and cultural preservation programs. In 1980, along with Christian social activist Peter Pond, he formed the Inter-Religious Mission for Peace in Cambodia. Together they located hundreds of surviving monks and nuns and helped them renew their vows and assume leadership roles in Cambodian temples throughout the world. With the support of Cambodian laypersons, Ghosananda founded over thirty temples in the U.S. and Canada alone. In Cambodia, he has helped rebuild many more temples, and he has led the movement to educate the monks and nuns in the skills of nonviolence and the monitoring of human rights.

In 1980, Maha Ghosananda accepted an invitation to represent the Khmer nation-in-exile as a consultant to the United Nations Economic and Social Council. From the UN, he launched many ecumenical initiatives, met frequently with the world's religious leaders, and helped create a prayerful awareness of Cambodia's suffering and the dire need for peace.

He also has led a contingency of monks to all of the top-level Cambodian peace talks, and, taking a strictly neutral stance, they have brought a calm presence to these meetings, proposing compromise, imploring the leaders to recall their Buddha nature, and reminding everyone of the power of nonviolence.

In 1988, Maha Ghosananda was elected *Somteja*, Supreme Patriarch of Cambodian Buddhism. Traditionally this important station would be confirmed by a popular vote of all Cambodian Buddhist monks, but because of the diaspora the appointment was determined by a small gathering of monks and lay leaders in Paris. Ghosananda lovingly accepts the leadership of his people, but he also says that he will resign when the sangha is reunited so that a universal election can take place.

Today Ghosananda continues to travel worldwide, bringing hope to his war-torn people and offering insight into the true nature of peace. In a recent conference with Norodom Sihanouk, now back in Cambodia as president of the interim government, Maha Ghosananda was assured that Buddhism will enjoy religious freedom and that human rights will be honored under the new government.

Much of the world is asking, "Is it right to allow the Khmer Rouge to participate in an interim government?" After years of witnessing the suffering of so many, Maha Ghosananda is still able to offer a serene smile and say, "We must have both wisdom and compassion. We condemn the act, but we cannot hate the actor. With our love, we will do everything we can to assure peace for all. There is no other way."

Over the years, many accolades have been offered to Maha
Ghosananda. He has been called the "Gandhi of Cambodia," "Cambodia's Living Treasure," and the "Living
Dharma." He is a man who offers loving kindness to the
world moment by moment: the humble teacher who rises
cheerfully to offer tea to his guests; the generous monk
who gives away almost everything that comes his way;
the temperate adept who shows no wanting or choosing;
the gentle *bodhisattva* who teaches through his beaming
face and sparkling laughter.

Step by Step is a collection of Maha Ghosananda's talks
and writings. Following in the footsteps of Gandhi and
embracing the deepest teachings of the Buddha, Ghosananda offers thoughts and insights into the nature of peace
and reconciliation, wisdom and compassion, and practices
for bringing them into our daily lives and into the glo-
bal community. This book was compiled with the help
of many friends and students of the Venerable Maha
Ghosananda. Working together, we shared two goals: to
thank the Venerable for the richness he has brought to our
lives, and to share his wisdom and compassion with a
wider audience. The editors gratefully acknowledge the
Reverend Thomas Ahlburn, of the First Unitarian-Univer-
salist Church of Providence, for his wise counsel and support; the late Frank Reed for his editorial and technical
advice and continuing inspiration; Sister Sophon So for
her patience, advice, and nourishing hospitality; Dr. David
Pugatch and Jesse Abbot for their countless hours of reading and research; and all the others whose many gifts have

helped make this book possible. We hope that we have succeeded in sharing Maha Ghosananda's boundless love and deep wisdom with our readers, and we hope that you will enjoy reading this slim volume again and again, discovering deeper and deeper layers of truth in his elegantly simple words.

Jane Mahoney and Philip Edmonds
Providence, Rhode Island
November 1991

Meditations on Wisdom

Prayer for Peace

Dear Brothers and Sisters, my name is Maha Ghosananda, and I am a Buddhist monk from Cambodia.

The people of Cambodia have known great suffering. I pray that, like millions of peaceful Cambodian people, all people will find strength and compassion in their hearts and guidance in these words of the Buddha:

> In those who harbor thoughts of blame and vengeance toward others, hatred will never cease. In those who do not harbor blame and vengeance, hatred will surely cease. For hatred is never appeased by hatred. Hatred is appeased by love. This is an eternal law.
>
> Just as a mother would protect her only child, even at the risk of her own life, so let one cultivate a boundless heart toward all beings. Let one's thoughts of love pervade the whole world—above, below, and across, without any obstruction, without any hatred, without any enmity.
>
> As long as one is awake, one should maintain this mindfulness. This is to obtain the blessed state in this very life.

The suffering of Cambodia has been deep.
From this suffering comes Great Compassion.
Great Compassion makes a Peaceful Heart.
A Peaceful Heart makes a Peaceful Person.
A Peaceful Person makes a Peaceful Family.
A Peaceful Family makes a Peaceful Community.
A Peaceful Community makes a Peaceful Nation.
And a Peaceful Nation makes a Peaceful World.
May all beings live in Happiness and Peace.

Amen.

To Rule the Universe

In the beginning, the gods and goddesses held an election to determine who would be best suited to rule the universe. The first candidate was Agnidevaputra, the God of Fire. "I am the strongest," he said, "so I should rule. Witness my power." Then, as he began to chant in a loud voice, a huge fire rose up from the center of the universe and began to burn everywhere. The other gods and goddesses trembled with fear, and they all raised their hands to elect Agnidevaputra. All, that is, except Valahakedeputra, the God of Water.

Valahakedeputra said, "I can control fire." And immediately he created a huge deluge to extinguish the fire. As the floodwaters rose higher and higher, all the deities raised their hands to vote for him, except Saradadevi, the Goddess of Art and Wisdom.

Saradadevi said, "Dear friends, fire and water can frighten and kill people, but I give birth to beauty. When I begin to dance, you will relax and completely forget about fire and water." Saradadevi then danced and sang, and all the gods and goddesses became entranced. Instead of drinking water through their mouths, they began pouring wine into their ears, eyes, and noses. Awed by Saradadevi's power, all of the deities raised their hands, except Gandharva, the God of Celestial Music.

Gandharva said, "Woman can overcome man, but man can also overcome woman." Then he began to play his heavenly guitar and sing, and all the deities swooned as the music flowed through the hall. As if in a stupor, they all raised their hands, except Santidevaputra, the God of Peace, Mindfulness, and Clear Comprehension.

Santidevaputra said, "I am the God of Peace. I always practice mindfulness and clear comprehension. Whether you vote for me or not, I rule myself. To rule the universe, you must first rule yourself. To rule yourself, you must be able to rule your own mind. To rule your mind, you must practice mindfulness and clear comprehension."

All of the gods and goddesses recognized Santidevaputra's strength and elected him unanimously. They understood that peace is the strongest force in the world.

One Teaching

There was once a young monk who studied assiduously every day, but he could not learn all of the scriptures and precepts. So he became distressed. He couldn't eat or sleep, and he grew weak and thin.

Finally, he approached the Buddha. "Lord, please take back my robe. There are many teachings, and I cannot master them all. I am not fit to be a monk."

The Buddha answered, "Do not worry. To be free, you must master only one thing."

"Please teach me," begged the monk. "If you give me just one practice, I will do it wholeheartedly, and I am sure that I can succeed."

So the Buddha told him, "Master the mind. When you have mastered the mind, you will know everything."

When we master the mind, we are free from all suffering. There is no need for any other teaching.

The Present Is Mother of the Future

We may notice that the vase of flowers on the table is very beautiful, but the flowers never tell us of their beauty. We never hear them boast of their sweet scent.

When a person has realized *nirvana*, it is the same. He or she does not have to say anything. We can sense his beauty, her sweetness, just by being there.

There is no need to worry about the past or the future. The secret of happiness is to be entirely present with what is in front of you, to live fully in the present moment. You can't go back and reshape the past. It's gone! You can't dictate the future. So there is no need to worry!

The next time I fly on an airplane, who knows what will happen? Maybe I will arrive safely, or maybe I won't. When we make plans, we can make them only in the present moment. This is the only moment we can control. We can love this moment and use it well. Past suffering can never harm us, if we truly care for the present.

Take care of the present, and the future will be well. The Dharma is always in the present, and the present is the mother of the future. Take care of the mother, and the mother will take care of her child.

Balancing Wisdom and Compassion

Wisdom must always be balanced by compassion, and compassion must be balanced by wisdom. We cannot have peace without this balance. I would like to share three stories to illustrate this.

One day, a violent dragon king met a bodhisattva on the path. The bodhisattva said, "My son, do not kill. If you keep the five precepts and care for all life, you will be happy." Hearing just these few words, the dragon became totally nonviolent.

The children who tended animals at the foot of the Himalayan mountains had been very afraid of the dragon. But when the dragon became gentle, they lost their fear and soon began to jump on him, pull his tail, and stuff stones and dirt into his mouth. After a while, the dragon could not eat, and he became very sick.

The next time the dragon king met the bodhisattva, he shouted, "You told me that if I kept the precepts and was compassionate, I would be happy. But now I suffer, and I am not happy at all."

The bodhisattva replied, "My son, if you have compassion, morality, and virtue, you must also have wisdom and intelligence. This is the way to protect yourself. The next time the children make you suffer, show them your fire. After that, they will trouble you no more."

Who was harmed when the dragon lacked wisdom? Both the dragon and the children suffered.

The balance of wisdom and compassion is called the middle path. Here is another story. Once an old farmer found a dying cobra in his ricefield. Seeing the cobra's suffering, the farmer was filled with compassion. He picked up the snake and carried him home. Then he fed the cobra warm milk, wrapped him in a soft blanket, and lovingly placed the snake beside him in his bed as he went to sleep. In the morning, the farmer was dead.

Why was he killed? Because he used only compassion and not wisdom. If you pick up a cobra, it will bite you. When you find a way to save the dying cobra without lifting it, you have balanced wisdom with compassion. Then you are happy, and the cobra is happy, too.

Here is the third story: There was a farmer who went into the forest with his friend to gather wood. When the farmer struck a tree with his axe, he disturbed a beehive, and a swarm of angry bees flew out and began stinging him.

The farmer's friend was filled with compassion. He grabbed his axe and killed the bees with swift, mighty blows. Unfortunately, he also killed the farmer.

Compassion without wisdom can cause great suffering. We might even say, "It is better to have a wise enemy than a foolish friend."

Wisdom and compassion must walk together. Having one without the other is like walking with one foot. You may hop a few times, but eventually you will fall. Balancing wisdom with compassion, you will walk very well—slowly and elegantly, step by step.

Letting Go of Suffering

The Buddha said, "I teach only two things—suffering and the end of suffering."

What is the cause of suffering? Suffering arises from clinging. If the mind says "I am," then there is suffering. If the mind says "I am not," then there is also suffering. As long as the mind clings, it suffers. When the mind is silent, it becomes peaceful and free.

Clinging has 108 names. It may be called greed, anger, envy, or covetousness. Clinging is like a snake that sheds its skin. Beneath one tough skin there is always another.

How can we be freed from suffering? We simply let it go. "Painfully we sustain it, happily we let it go." Suffering follows one with an untamed mind as surely as a cart follows an ox. Peacefulness follows one who has mastered the mind as surely as his own shadow.

Clinging always brings suffering. This is a natural law, like the law of fire. It does not matter whether you believe that fire is hot. When you hold fire, it will burn you.

The Dharma teaches us to know, shape, and free the mind. When the mind is mastered, all of the Dharma is mastered. What is the key for mastering the mind? It is mindfulness.

Does it take long to be released from suffering? No, enlightenment is always here and now. But to realize this may take many lifetimes!

The Middle Path

The road to peace is called the middle path. It is beyond all duality and all opposites. Sometimes it is called equanimity. Equanimity harmonizes all extremes. Equanimity is like the finely-tuned string of an instrument, not too tight and not too loose. It vibrates perfectly and makes beautiful music.

Equanimity means the absence of struggle. One time a great elephant jumped into a mud hole to cool off. Of course he got stuck, and the more he struggled, the deeper he sank! Struggling is useless. It only makes things worse. Do not struggle with suffering. Find your own path. This is called taking refuge in the Dharma. The Dharma is the middle path.

Before the Buddha began his spiritual journey, he indulged in many kinds of sensual pleasure, but he found no lasting happiness. After that, he fasted for many weeks, until he became pale and thin, but he found only pain. Practicing in this way, the Buddha learned that both self-indulgence and self-mortification are extremes, and extremes can never bring happiness.

Peace comes only when we stop struggling with opposites. The middle path has no beginning and no end, so we do not need to travel far on the middle path to find peace. The middle path is not only the road *to* peace, it is also the road *of* peace. It is very safe, and very pleasant to travel.

Good Luck, Bad Luck

Opposites are endless. Good and bad, day and night, right and wrong, mine and yours, praising and blaming—all are opposites, all are endless.

Opposites produce each other. Day becomes night, and death becomes rebirth. The egg becomes the hen, and the hen makes the egg. In just this way, good luck and bad luck are an endless cycle.

There was once a farmer who lost his mare. When the mare disappeared, the people of the village said, "Bad luck!" But when the mare came home the very next day followed by a good strong horse, the people of the village said, "Good luck!" Yesterday they thought "bad luck," today they think "good luck." Yesterday they said "loss," but today they say "gain." Which is true? Gain and loss are opposites.

When the farmer's son rode the beautiful horse, he fell and broke his leg. Then all of the people said, "Bad luck!" War came, and all of the strong men were drafted. Many men fought and died on the battlefield. Because the farmer's son had broken his leg, he could not go to war. Was this loss or gain? Good luck or bad luck? Who knows?

We Must Eat Time

What is life? Life is eating and drinking through all of our senses. And life is keeping from being eaten. What eats us? Time! What is time? Time is living in the past or living in the future, feeding on the emotions. Beings who can say that they have been mentally healthy for even one minute are rare in the world. Most of us suffer from clinging to pleasant, unpleasant, and neutral feelings, and from hunger and thirst. Most living beings have to eat and drink every second through their eyes, ears, nose, tongue, skin, and nerves. We eat twenty-four hours a day without stopping! We crave food for the body, food for feeling, food for volitional action, and food for rebirth. We are what we eat. We are the world, and we eat the world.

The Buddha cried when he saw this endless cycle of suffering: the fly eats the flower; the frog eats the fly; the snake eats the frog; the bird eats the snake; the tiger eats the bird; the hunter kills the tiger; the tiger's body becomes swollen; flies come and eat the tiger's corpse; the flies lay eggs in the corpse; the eggs become more flies; the flies eat the flowers; and the frogs eat the flies....

And so the Buddha said, "I teach only two things—suffering and the end of suffering." Suffering, eating, and feeling are exactly the same.

Feeling eats everything. Feeling has six mouths—the eye, ear, nose, tongue, body, and mind. The first mouth eats forms through the eye. The second mouth eats sound. The third mouth eats smells. The fourth mouth eats tastes. The fifth mouth eats physical contact. And the last mouth eats ideas. That is feeling.

Time is also an eater. In traditional Cambodian stories, there is often a giant with many mouths who eats everything. This giant is time. If you eat time, you gain nirvana. You can eat time by living in the moment. When you live just in this moment, time cannot eat you.

Everything is causational. There is no you, only causes and conditions. Therefore, *you* cannot hear or see. When sound and ear come together, there is hearing. When form and eye meet, there is seeing.

When eye, form, and consciousness meet, there is eye contact. Eye contact conditions feeling. Feeling conditions perception. Perception conditions thinking, and thinking is I, my, me—the painful misconception that I see, hear, smell, taste, touch, and think.

Feeling uses the eye to eat shapes. If a shape is beautiful, a pleasant feeling enters the eye. If a shape is not beautiful, it brings an unpleasant feeling. If we are not attentive to a shape, a neutral feeling comes. The ear is the same: sweet sounds bring pleasant feelings, harsh sounds bring unpleasant feelings, and inattention brings neutral feelings.

Again, you may think, "I am seeing, I am hearing, I am feeling." But it is not you, it is only contact, the meeting of the eye, form, and eye-consciousness. It is only the Dharma.

A man once asked the Buddha, "Who feels?" The Buddha answered, "This is not a real question." No one feels. Feeling feels. There is no I, my, or me. There is only the Dharma.

All kinds of feelings are suffering, filled with vanity, filled with "I am." If we can penetrate the nature of sensations, we can realize the pure happiness of nirvana.

Feelings and sensations cause us to suffer, because we fail to realize that they are impermanent. The Buddha asked, "How can feeling be permanent if it depends upon the body, which is impermanent?" When we do not control our feelings, we are controlled by them. If we live in the moment, we can see things just as they are. Doing so, we can put an end to all desire, break our bondage, and realize peace.

To understand pleasant, unpleasant, and neutral feelings, we have to put the four foundations of mindfulness into practice. Mindfulness can transform pleasant, unpleasant, and neutral feelings into wisdom.

The world is created by the mind. If we can control feeling, then we can control the mind. If we can control the mind, then we can rule the world.

In meditation, we relax our body, but we sit up straight, and, by following our breathing or another object of concentration, we stop most of our thinking. Therefore, we stop being pushed around by our feelings. Thinking creates feeling, and feeling creates thinking. To be free from clinging to thinking and feeling is nirvana—the highest, supreme happiness.

To live without suffering means to live always in the present. The highest happiness is here and now. There is no time at all unless we cling to it. Brothers and Sisters, please eat time!

The Bodhi Tree

The Bodhi tree is the tree of life. When the Buddha sat under the Bodhi tree for many weeks in quiet contemplation, he gained enlightenment. You can find a Bodhi tree anywhere, in Cambodia, in India, even in your own backyard.

The Bodhi tree is called "the great tree of life" because all that is needed for lasting peace can be found in its roots, trunk, branches, and fruit. The Bodhi tree is a beautiful symbol for Buddhism.

We can begin to learn about the Bodhi tree at its roots, which are known as the roots of all actions. Three roots are wholesome, and so they naturally bear sweet fruits—generosity, wisdom, and loving kindness. The other three are unwholesome, and so they naturally bear bitter fruits—greed, hatred, and delusion.

The roots of the Bodhi tree extend into the trunk, which is made up of five aggregates—form, feeling, perception, mental formation, and consciousness. These are the components of all physical and mental phenomena, the basic elements of all our experience. The five aggregates are all slaves to feeling. They are like cooks preparing food for feeling to eat through the eye, the ear, the nose, the tongue, the body, and the mind. We can meditate on the five aggregates, making them the objects of our mindfulness. To live mindfully is to live without clinging to any of them.

The trunk of the Bodhi tree grows into twelve branches which are links in the great chain of dependent origination. The Buddha saw that this chain was the cause of our painful cycle of birth and death. The branches of the Bodhi tree teach us that everything in life arises through causes and conditions. Ignorance conditions volitional actions, which condition consciousness, which conditions the mind and body, which condition the six sense doors—eyes, ears, nose, tongue, body, and mind—which condition contact between a sense door and a sense object, which conditions feeling. All feeling—pleasant, unpleasant, or neutral—is suffering, because feeling is impermanent. When we are not mindful, feeling goes on to condition craving or aversion, which conditions clinging, which conditions the karmic formations of becoming, which condition rebirth, which conditions the entire cycle of birth and death once again.

The Bodhi tree teaches us how to break this endless chain of suffering. The secret is mindfulness. If we use mindfulness to observe and control feeling, then clinging cannot arise. If clinging does not arise, then suffering cannot arise. It is really very simple. We can learn mindfulness step by step, throughout our lifetime.

Nirvana

A wise Unitarian minister asked me, "Where is nirvana? Can people still reach nirvana these days?" I answered, "Nirvana is here and now."

Nirvana is everywhere. It dwells in no particular place. It is in the mind. It can only be found in the present moment.

Nirvana is the absence of suffering. It is empty and void of concept. Nothing can comprise nirvana. Nirvana is beyond cause and effect. Nirvana is the highest happiness. It is absolute peace. Peace in the world depends on conditions, but peace in nirvana is unchanging.

Nirvana is the absence of karma, the fruits of our actions. Karma can follow us through many lifetimes. When we die, karma becomes like a flame passing from one candle to another. In the state of nirvana there is no clinging, no expectation, and no desire. Each moment is fresh, new, and innocent. All karma is erased, just as we erase the tape in a tape recorder.

Suffering leads the way to nirvana. When we truly understand suffering, we become free.

Body Sick, Mind Well

The nature of the human body is to grow old and decline. Yet even as the body weakens or is harmed by an opponent, the mind can remain clear. Even in the midst of pain, the mind can be at peace.

The body is a vehicle, like a car, a plane, or a bicycle. We use the body, but we need not allow it to use us. If we can control the mind, then even when we are faced with physical suffering it can remain free and clear.

The Buddha said, "Care for your health. It is the foundation of all progress." When we feel physical pain, we Cambodians like to say, "The body may be sick, but the mind is very well!"

Dharmayana

The Dharma is good in the beginning, good in the middle, and good in the end. Good in the beginning is the goodness of the moral precepts— not to kill, steal, commit adultery, tell lies, or take intoxicants. Good in the middle is concentration. Good in the end is wisdom and nirvana.

The Dharma is visible here and now. It is always in the present, the omnipresent. The Dharma is timeless. It offers results at once.

In Buddhism, there are three *yanas,* or vehicles, and none is higher or better than any other. All three carry the same Dharma. But there is a fourth vehicle that is even more complete. I call it *Dharmayana,* the universe itself, and it includes every way that leads to peace and loving kindness. Because it is complete, Dharmayana can never be sectarian. It can never divide us from any of our brothers or sisters.

Come and experience it for yourself. The Dharma vehicle will bring you to nirvana right here and now. Step by step, moment by moment, it is comprehensible and can be understood by anyone. Dharmayana is the kind of Buddhism I love.

Mindfulness and Clear Comprehension

Mindfulness protects us. As the mind grows clear and still, it can no longer be driven by ignorance or desire. Mindfulness is the driver of the chariot of the Dharma.

"Gathering in" is the characteristic quality of mindfulness. We gather in all that we observe. "Cutting out" is the characteristic quality of clear comprehension. We discard all except the precise object of our concentration. Mindfulness gathers in the hindrances of the mind, and clear comprehension follows to cut the hindrances out.

Mindfulness and clear comprehension are at the heart of Buddhist meditation. Peace is realized when we are mindful in each and every step. Through mindfulness, we can protect ourselves, and we also protect the whole world.

The Buddha's last words were offered for our protection. "Be mindful," he told his disciples, in exactly the same way that we often remind our loved ones to "take care."

Meditations on Compassion

Making Peace

Non-action is the source of all action. There is little we can do for peace in the world without peace in our minds. And so, when we begin to make peace, we begin with silence—meditation and prayer.

Peacemaking requires compassion. It requires the skill of listening. To listen, we have to give up ourselves, even our own words. We listen until we can hear our peaceful nature. As we learn to listen to ourselves, we learn to listen to others as well, and new ideas grow. There is an openness, a harmony. As we come to trust one another, we discover new possibilities for resolving conflicts. When we listen well, we will hear peace growing.

Peacemaking requires mindfulness. There is no peace with jealousy, self-righteousness, or meaningless criticism. We must decide that making peace is more important than making war.

Peacemaking requires selflessness. It is selflessness taking root. To make peace, the skills of teamwork and cooperation are essential. There is little we can do for peace as long as we feel that we are the only ones who know the way. A real peacemaker will strive only for peace, not for fame, glory, or even honor. Striving for fame, glory, or honor will only harm our efforts.

Peacemaking requires wisdom. Peace is a path that is chosen consciously. It is not an aimless wandering, but a step-by-step journey.

Peacemaking is the middle path of equanimity, non-duality, and non-attachment. Peacemaking means the perfect balance of wisdom and compassion, and the perfect meeting of humanitarian needs and political realities. It means compassion without concession, and peace without appeasement.

Loving kindness is the only way to peace.

Think Before You Speak

The thought manifests as the word.
The word manifests as the deed.
The deed develops into the habit.
The habit hardens into the character.
The character gives birth to the destiny.
So, watch your thoughts with care
And let them spring from love
Born out of respect for all beings.

Great Compassion

If I am good to someone, he or she will learn goodness and, in turn, will be good to others. If I am not good, he or she will harbor hatred and resentment and will, in turn, pass it on to others. If the world is not good, I have to make more effort to be good myself.

Taking care of others is the same as taking care of myself. When I respect and serve others, I am serving all Buddhas everywhere. This is called great compassion. Compassion is a happy mental state.

When we protect ourselves through mindfulness, we are protecting others as well. When we protect other living beings through compassionate action, we are also protecting ourselves.

No Boundaries to Loving Kindness

There is nothing more glorious than peace. When we stabilize our posture and calm our mind, we can realize peace within ourselves. Then we can radiate loving kindness to those around us—our family, our community, our nation, and the whole world.

We can meditate like this: "May I be happy. May I be peaceful. May I be free from anger. May I be free from suffering."

Why must we love ourselves first? Because peace begins with the individual. It is only by loving ourselves first that we are able to extend love to others. Charity begins at home. By protecting ourselves, we protect the whole world. By loving ourselves, we love the whole world. When we say, "May I be happy," we are speaking for everyone. The whole world is one. Life is one. We are all of the same Buddha nature.

Loving kindness is a very powerful energy. It radiates to all beings, without distinction. It radiates to our loved ones, to those toward whom we feel indifferent, and to our enemies. There are no boundaries to loving kindness. The Dharma is founded in loving kindness. The Buddha saw the whole world with compassion. And so, our prayer for personal happiness naturally grows into a prayer for everyone, "May the whole world be happy and free from suffering."

Buddhist scriptures describe the merits of loving kindness meditation. They tell us that those who practice loving kindness sleep well. They have no bad dreams. They wake up happy. They can focus their minds quickly. Their minds are clear and calm. They have no nervousness. No fire, poisons, or weapons will harm them. They can solve all the problems of the world. They are loved by all sentient beings. Their complexion becomes clear. They will attain nirvana. Altogether, there are fifty-two blessings derived from meditating on loving kindness.

When we love all beings, we gain the blessing of fearlessness. Our speech and all of our physical and mental actions become clear, and we become free.

The greatest happiness is found in living without egoism. This is one of the fruits of loving kindness. Another is contentment with life as it is. Life often seems burdensome, but it becomes easy when we stop struggling. Moment after moment, step by step, we can experience life as something light and pleasant. There is no need to hurry!

With loving kindness, we are like a fish in clear water, never submerged by the burdens of the world. We float down the stream of time, easily, from moment to moment. We have complete peace in our eyes, ears, nose, tongue, body, and mind, because we control all of our senses. We have clear comprehension about the purpose of our life and about how to live happily. We also have clear comprehension about the object of our concentration and about I, my, and me. The Buddha said, "There is no I, my, or me," and this becomes clear when we put loving kindness into practice.

Typically, we are selfish about our family, money, dwelling, name, and fame, and also about the Dharma. But when we put loving kindness into practice, we become generous. We give food, money, shelter, and the Dharma freely to all.

Loving kindness also means friendliness. With loving kindness, all enmity is transformed. Our enemies will no longer hate us and, eventually, they will return our loving kindness to us, as friends.

Yes, my friends, that is loving kindness.

Anger

When anger controls us, we harm ourselves and the people around us. Anger burns the mind and the body. The face becomes flushed, the heart weakens, and the hands tremble.

Our first duty is to protect ourselves, so we say, "May I be free from harming myself, may I be free from anger." Then we say, "May I be free from harming others, may I be free from anger." When we analyze anger, we find that it has no substance of its own. It is always conditioned by something else. There is no "I" to be angry. There is only the Dharma.

When we are angry, our face becomes ugly. Anger is fire, and it burns hundreds of cells in our brain and in our blood.

If we have loving kindness, our faces become brilliant, radiant, and beautiful. Loving kindness is like water. If we leave boiling water sitting for some time, it naturally becomes cool again. Sometimes we may boil with anger, but we can cool down gracefully by contemplating loving kindness, anger's opposite. The nature of water is to cleanse. When the mind is angry, it becomes soiled. Using the water of loving kindness, we can cleanse our mind. Like water, loving kindness flows everywhere.

"Bodhi" means to wake up, to see things as they are. When we wake up to our anger, it loses all of its force. Then anger gives birth to its opposite—compassion, the compassionate heart of the Buddha.

Universal Love

Many religious leaders preach that theirs is the only way to salvation. I listen with a smile, but I do not agree.

Two thousand five hundred years ago, the Buddha told his disciple Kalama,

> Do not accept anything simply because it has
>   been said by your teacher,
> Or because it has been written in your sacred
>   book,
> Or because it has been believed by many,
> Or because it has been handed down by your
>   ancestors.
> Accept and live only according to what will en-
>   able you to see truth face to face.

At our Providence temple we have a good friend called "Bodhisattva," who teaches English to the monks. Bodhisattva is a wise and patient teacher, but he also has a great challenge—he stutters when he speaks.

One day Bodhisattva was giving the monks a lesson. "H-h-house," he said. And all of the monks repeated exactly, "H-h-house!" Bodhisattva was startled. "N-n-no!" he said. And all of the monks said "N-n-no!" in unison.

Bodhisattva showed the monks the way to enlightenment. Truth is not just what we hear. We cannot know truth from teachers, books, or dogma only. The Buddha advises us to test the truth on the touchstone of our experience. Truth can be known only through our own mindful experience.

No religion is higher than truth. Our goal as humans is to realize our universal brotherhood and sisterhood. I pray that this realization will be spread throughout our troubled world. I pray that we can learn to support each other in our quest for peace.

Giving

Jesus said, "Whatsoever you have given to one of my brothers, you have given to me as well."

Great beings maintain their mental balance by giving preference to the welfare of others, working to alleviate the suffering of others, feeling joy for the successes of others, and treating all beings equally.

Great beings receive their pleasure in giving gifts. To avoid harming others, they practice the five precepts. They practice non-indulgence in order to perfect their virtue. They practice meditation in order to see clearly what is good and what is not good for beings.

Great beings constantly arouse their energy by keeping the welfare of others at heart. When they attain great courage through this exertion of energy, they become patient with others' faults. They do not deceive. They are unshakeably committed to the welfare and happiness of others. With loving kindness, they always place the welfare of others before their own. With equanimity, they expect no reward. This is how they perfect all the good states, beginning with giving.

We Are Our Temple

Many Buddhists are suffering—in Tibet, Cambodia, Laos, Burma, Vietnam, and elsewhere. The most important thing we Buddhists can do is to foster the liberation of the human spirit in every nation of the human family. We must use our religious heritage as a living resource.

What can Buddhism do to heal the wounds of the world? What did the Buddha teach that we can use to heal and elevate the human condition? One of the Buddha's most courageous acts was to walk onto a battlefield to stop a conflict. He did not sit in his temple waiting for the opponents to approach him. He walked right onto the battlefield to stop the conflict. In the West, we call this "conflict resolution."

How do we resolve a conflict, a battle, a power struggle? What does reconciliation really mean? Gandhi said that the essence of nonviolent action is that it seeks to put an end to antagonism, not the antagonists. This is important. The opponent has our respect. We implicitly trust his or her human nature and understand that ill-will is caused by ignorance. By appealing to the best in each other, both of us achieve the satisfaction of peace. We both become peacemakers. Gandhi called this a "bilateral victory."

We Buddhists must find the courage to leave our temples and enter the temples of human experience, temples that are filled with suffering. If we listen to the Buddha, Christ, or Gandhi, we can do nothing else. The refugee camps, the prisons, the ghettos, and the battlefields will then become our temples. We have so much work to do.

This will be a slow transformation, for many people throughout Asia have been trained to rely on the traditional monkhood. Many Cambodians tell me, "Venerable, monks belong in the temple." It is difficult for them to adjust to this new role, but we monks must answer the increasingly loud cries of suffering. We only need to remember that our temple is with us always. We *are* our temple.

Peace Is Growing Slowly

There is no self. There are only causes and conditions. Therefore, to struggle with ourselves and others is useless. The wise ones know that the root causes and conditions of all conflicts are in the mind.

Victory creates hatred. Defeat creates suffering. The wise ones wish for neither victory nor defeat.

We can oppose selfishness with the weapon of generosity. We can oppose ignorance with the weapon of wisdom. We can oppose hatred with the weapon of loving kindness.

The Buddha said, "When we are wronged, we must set aside all resentment and say, 'My mind will not be disturbed. Not one angry word will escape from my lips. I will remain kind and friendly, with loving thoughts and no secret malice.'" Peace begins in the mind. Yes, we show loving kindness, even for the oppressor.

After a great darkness, we see the dawning of peace in Cambodia. We are grateful for the Buddha's compassion and light, his realization of peace, unity, and wisdom. We pray that this unity, the heart of reconciliation, the middle path, will be present at every meeting and dialogue of Cambodia's leaders.

We seek to learn and teach the skills of peace. When we live the Dharma, we develop inner peace and the outer skills needed to make peace a reality. With peacemakers of all faiths, we can accept no victory except peace itself. We have no need for personal honor, title, or glory.

Loving kindness is alive in every heart. Listen carefully. Peace is growing in Cambodia, slowly, step by step.

Self-Determination

The suffering of Cambodia is but a mirror of the suffering of the world. The Buddha tells us that enlightenment begins when we realize that life is suffering.

This may seem negative or pessimistic to many people, but it is not. It is only a statement of our shared circumstance, to be seen without regret or attachment.

Mahatma Gandhi said that our suffering is a path to self-purification. He said, "When the *satyagraha* practices *ahimsa* and suffers voluntarily, the love that develops within has a tremendous power. It affects and elevates everyone around, including the opponent." Gandhi called this "The Law of Suffering." The Buddha also taught that suffering teaches us compassion. Whenever I think about the suffering of the Cambodian people, I am filled with compassion.

The Buddha said, "You must work out your own salvation with diligence." What does this mean? Each of us is responsible for our own salvation. This is self-determination in its purest, most essential form. All understanding of liberation, personal or national, must begin with this point.

The idea of personal salvation has been debated among different religions and schools of thought. Personal salvation does not mean salvation exclusive of the rest of humanity. If we follow the eightfold path, the path toward an end to suffering, our growing union with the universal spirit unfolds naturally, and our love comes to embrace all living beings. Personal salvation is but a microcosm of human salvation.

If we meditate on the ten perfections, we gradually become selfless, and we cannot help but inspire those around us. Gandhi said, "The satyagraha seeks self-realization through social service." The Dalai Lama recently told me, "To exterminate the root cause of all suffering, we must seek refuge in the three precious gems—the Buddha, the Dharma, and the Sangha. We must develop altruism and a strong will." He said that it is his firm belief that this will bring lasting peace and happiness to the entire human race.

The key to social service and social ethics is loving kindness. Loving kindness is no different from ahimsa, nonharming. It includes the well-being of everyone. According to the Buddha, even when our body is dismembered we can radiate good will toward all beings, remaining patient toward those who caused the harm and causing them no injury, even in thought. Hatred is never appeased by hatred. Hatred is only appeased by love.

Who Is the Enemy?

In 1981, the United Nations held a conference to discuss the future of Cambodia. During that time, we held a Buddhist ceremony for peace. At the end of the ceremony, a Khmer Rouge leader came up to me, very cautiously, and asked if I would come to Thailand to build a temple at the border. I said that I would.

"Oh!" thought many people, "he is talking to the enemy. He is helping the enemy! How can he do that?" I reminded them that love embraces all beings, whether they are noble-minded or low-minded, good or evil.

Both the noble and the good are embraced because loving kindness flows to them spontaneously. The unwholesome-minded must be included because they are the ones who need loving kindness the most. In many of them, the seed of goodness may have died because warmth was lacking for its growth. It perished from coldness in a world without compassion.

Gandhi said that he was always ready to compromise. He said, "Behind my non-cooperation there is always the keenest desire to cooperate, on the slightest pretext, even with the worst of opponents. To me, a very imperfect mortal is ever in need of God's grace, ever in need of the Dharma. No one is beyond redemption."

I do not question that loving one's oppressors—Cambodians loving the Khmer Rouge—may be the most difficult attitude to achieve. But it is a law of the universe that retaliation, hatred, and revenge only continue the cycle and never stop it. Reconciliation does not mean that we surrender rights and conditions, but rather that we use love in all of our negotiations. It means that we see ourselves in the opponent—for what is the opponent but a being in ignorance, and we ourselves are also ignorant of many things. Therefore, only loving kindness and right mindfulness can free us.

Gandhi said, "The more you develop ahimsa in your being, the more infectious it becomes, until it overwhelms your surroundings and, by and by, it might oversweep this world!" We are each individually responsible for our own salvation and our own happiness. Through our service, we find a road to salvation. This service is nothing but our love for all beings and the uplifting of ignorance into light.

The Human Family

During his lifetime, the Buddha lobbied for peace and human rights. We can learn much from a lobbyist like him.

Human rights begin when each man becomes a brother and each woman becomes a sister, when we honestly care for each other. Then Cambodians will help Jews, and Jews will help Africans, and Africans will help others. We will all become servants for each others' rights.

It is so even in my tiny country. Until Cambodians are concerned with Vietnam's right to exist and be free, and with Thailand's rights, and even with China's rights, we will be denied our own rights.

When we accept that we are part of a great human family—that every man and every woman has the nature of Buddha, Allah, and Christ—then we will sit, talk, make peace, and bring humankind to its fullest flowering.

I pray that all of us will realize peace in this lifetime, and save all beings from suffering!

Peacemaking is at the heart of life. We peacemakers must meet as often as possible to make peace in ourselves, our countries, and the whole world.

Any real peace will not favor East, West, North, or South. A peaceful Cambodia will be friendly to all. Peace is nonviolent, and so we Cambodians will remain nonviolent toward all as we rebuild our country. Peace is based on justice and freedom, and so a peaceful Cambodia will be just and free.

Our journey for peace begins today and every day. Making peace is our life. We must invite people from around the world to join in our journey. As we make peace for ourselves and our country, we make peace for the whole world.

Preserving Our Heritage

North America is a melting pot. We Cambodians have been here for just one generation. In recent years, we have also resettled in Europe, Australia, and throughout Asia. As we rebuild our lives in new lands, as we become part of new societies, it is important for us also to preserve our cultural identity. Without our culture, we will become lost and confused, like fish out of water.

Cambodians have a precious heritage. The richness of Cambodian culture includes many gifts:

> Cambodians are fearless because they can overcome greed, anger, and delusion.
>
> Cambodians are humble, courteous, and noble.
>
> Cambodians are grateful to their mothers and fathers, to their leaders, to their land, and to the whole world.
>
> Cambodians keep the five moral precepts, the constitution of humanity, and the Dharma of goodness.
>
> Cambodians have mindfulness and clear comprehension as their protectors.
>
> Cambodians practice loving kindness, compassion, sympathetic joy, and equanimity.
>
> Cambodians have patience. They can bear great difficulties, suffering, and hardships.

Cambodians forgive and forget the wrongs of
   other people. They learn from the lessons of
   the past. They use the present to build the
   future.
Cambodians are truthful and well-behaved.
   They follow the middle path.
Cambodians are soft and smiling. Their speech
   is truthful, loving, and practical, clear, vi-
   brant, and sweet. Their speech has the power
   to free the mind from anxiety, to purify the
   mind from delusion, and to make the mind
   strong.
Cambodians have the tradition of solidarity,
   united by Buddhism and their love of
   Dharma.

When we are in the river, we flow with the river, zig-zag.
But we cannot forget our boat, which is our tradition. As
Buddhas all, may the Cambodian people be peacemakers.
In the tradition of our sacred land, may we celebrate unity,
loving kindness, and peace with our deepest gratitude.

Building Bridges

Cambodia has been torn by death, starvation, and strife. Our people have turned against each other, brother fighting brother. The whole world has been supplying guns to our people to help us kill one another.

Now we are brought to our one common element—the middle path of the Dharma. There is no other path for us. We must travel the middle path together, step by step. On our journey, we seek to awaken the Buddha nature, the Christ nature, the burning light of peace in all our people. We seek to awaken the nonviolent nature of Cambodians. War, guns, and fighting have caused us terrible suffering. Now it is time for peace, for a nonviolent resolution to all of our problems. We seek to rebuild the sangha, the Cambodian Buddhist community. We want to support Buddhist monks and nuns and to help temples grow in Cambodia and throughout the world. We seek to rebuild the bridges among our people, no matter how grave the differences may seem.

We are united by our own Buddha nature, and with our Buddha nature we can build bridges of unity, understanding, and peace. We will journey to Cambodia and to every corner of the world where there are Cambodians. Each step will be a prayer, and each step will build a bridge. Our pilgrimage is one with all the world's religions and with all the world's religious leaders. Each person's prayer and meditation is a powerful vibration of peace for Cambodia and the entire world.

Four Faces, One Heart

During the Angkor period of our history, the ancient kings built elaborate temples. These stone temples reached to the skies and extended for miles, and so they were called "temple mountains." One of the most famous is Angkor Thom. Parts of Angkor Thom still stand today.

At Angkor Thom's main gate, there is a beautiful sculpture. It is a very large head with four faces of the Buddha, gazing out in four directions. The faces stand for great qualities of the Buddha—loving kindness, compassion, equanimity, and sympathetic joy.

Why has this sculpture endured for so many centuries? Because it holds a promise—the nearly-forgotten secret to peace in Cambodia: loving kindness, compassion, equanimity, and sympathetic joy. Four faces, one heart. Four factions, one Cambodia. Peace is coming slowly, step by step.

An Army of Peace

Listory is being made. Four armies are putting down their guns. Four factions are joining to govern. We are all walking together.

All Cambodia weeps for the dead. Every act has a consequence. Years of violence have brought great tragedy. More violence can only bring only more harm.

Now is the time for peace, and Buddhist monks will bring a fifth army to Cambodia—the army of the Buddha. We will shoot the people with bullets of loving kindness.

The army of the Buddha will maintain strict neutrality. Mindfulness will be our armor. We will be an army of so much courage that we will turn away from violence. Our goal will be to bring an end to suffering.

We will work for unity, freedom, and for an international policy of friendship. In the days ahead, we will continue to broaden the spiritual ground for peace. We will continue to strengthen our skills for peace. We will seek to organize ourselves as an army of peace.

As we go forward, let us remember these seven basic principles:

1. Cambodia embraces a distinctive people, culture, and religious tradition that must be preserved and maintained.
2. Cambodian people overwhelmingly desire nonviolence, disarmament, and neutrality.

3. Cambodian people must obtain all basic human rights, including rights of self-determination and rights to freely pursue economic, social, and cultural development.
4. Nonviolence is the primary precept of Cambodian history, culture, and religion.
5. Cambodian people everywhere need to be invited to join in this meditation and peace effort.
6. Buddhism offers a reconciling, universal, and unifying spirit.
7. The way of the eightfold path—right understanding, right mindfulness, right speech, right action, right livelihood, right effort, right attention, right concentration—will bring peace.

May the richness and power of our heritage, the goodness of Cambodians everywhere, and the wisdom and compassion of the Buddha move us to a peaceful reunification.

Love's Embrace

Cambodian people have a special way of greeting each other. They cup their hands in a prayerful pose and bow their heads low. This is called *sompeah*, "I bow to your Buddha nature."

When Cambodians greet persons of special importance, they offer a long and warm embrace. Then they gently lift the honored one into the air. This gesture places the honored one's head above the head of the greeter. It says, "I have deep reverence for your being."

When I met Pope John Paul II on the Vatican steps, we shared a warm embrace. Then, to show respect, I tried to lift him. But I am a small monk and the Pope is of great stature. My arm was sore for weeks afterwards. Compassion must be met with wisdom!

Some people say that Buddhism and Christianity cannot live together. I say, "Why not?" Love can embrace everything.

I bring love to the Pope, the Pope is happy. He embraces me, and I embrace him. We are fearless together because of love.

Each Step Is a Prayer

The Buddha called the practice of mindfulness "the only way." Always in the present. At this very moment. From moment to moment. In all activity. In this very step.

This is why we say, "Step by step. Each step is a meditation." When the children in Providence see me off at the station, as I walk up to the train, they shout, "Slowly, slowly, step by step, each step is a prayer!" and all the passengers look and smile. This saying has become famous!

The children do not know English well, but they know this sentence by heart. They are the new Cambodia, and already they know the way to peace.

In Cambodia, we say, "A journey of 10,000 miles begins with a single step."

Slowly, slowly, step by step. Each step is a meditation. Each step is a prayer.

Inter-Religious Mission for Peace in Cambodia

The Inter-Religious Mission for Peace in Cambodia is a non-profit organization dedicated to rebuilding Cambodian Buddhism and to promoting peace and human rights. Donations are gratefully accepted. For more information, please contact Philip Edmonds, c/o Amos House, P.O. Box 2873, Providence, RI 02907.

Worldwide Centers

178 Hanover Street
Providence, RI 02907, U.S.A.
401-273-0969

12 bis Rue de la Liberté
9220 Bagneaux, France
33-41-46635717

1 Meinrad Strasse
CH-8006, Zürich, Switzerland
41-1-363-5900

96/2 Soi St. Louis
Bangkok 10120, Thailand
66-2-211-6456

7210 De Nancy
Montreal, Quebec H3R 2L7, Canada
514-735-6901

Parallax Press publishes books and tapes on mindful awareness and social responsibility, "making peace right in the moment we are alive." It is our hope that doing so will help create a more peaceful world. Some of our recent books include:

Being Peace, by Thich Nhat Hanh

The Path of Compassion: Writings on Socially Engaged Buddhism, edited by Fred Eppsteiner

In the Footsteps of Gandhi: Conversations with Spiritual Social Activists, by Catherine Ingram

Worlds in Harmony: Dialogues on Compassionate Action, by His Holiness the Dalai Lama

Seeds of Peace: A Buddhist Vision for Renewing Society, by Sulak Sivaraksa

World As Lover, World As Self, by Joanna Macy

Dharma Gaia: A Harvest of Essays in Buddhism and Ecology, edited by Allan Hunt Badiner

For a copy of our free catalog, please write to:
Parallax Press
P.O. Box 7355
Berkeley, CA 94707